Ralph's Rough Rules for Success

Ten Simple Rules for Success and Satisfaction in the Business World

Copyright 2018, All rights Reserved

Version 1.0

Table of Contents

1. **All jobs are temporary.**

    In this day and age, this should be self-evident.

2. **It pays by the hour.**

    If it doesn't, watch out!

3. **Go for the money.**

    They know what the job is worth!

4. **You never know who your next boss (or company) will be.**

    If you don't like your boss or company, wait a minute!

5. **Be willing to change anything.**

    Except maybe your sex!

6. **Negotiate, negotiate, negotiate; everything is negotiable.**

Well, almost everything.

7. **Unwritten rules are more important than written rules.**

    Conformance with the corporate culture is everything. In fact, the written rules are frequently meaningless!

8. **Get the big picture.**

    We live in an international corporate world, be international in outlook.

9. **Take all difficult assignments.**

    It will look good on your resume even if success was not possible.

10. **Always have a plan B, and a plan C, and a plan D, etc.!**

    Go on to bigger and better things, or, if at first you do not succeed, try, try, again (usually somewhere else).

Epilogue – Murphy's Laws

Authors Information

Chapter 1

All jobs are temporary.

In this day and age, this should be self-evident.

Many years ago I worked for a company in a job that I dearly loved and enjoyed. I would probably still be there today if conditions had been different. Unfortunately, the company underwent several mergers and then experienced a sudden and sharp downturn in its sales. Layoffs began starting at the top; the company president was the first to go. At the end of each day one or more persons would be called into their bosses office and would be given the bad news. The next morning there were announcements on the bulletin board that so and so had "resigned." It became a joke that employees should check the bulletin board when they came in each morning to see if they had "resigned" the previous evening.

This chapter hardly needs to be written for most people because in this day and age. The statement that "all jobs are temporary" should be self-evident. However, this chapter was written for the rest of the people for whom the concept is not self evident, to reinforce this concept for those who already know it, and to add bulk to the book. When writing books it pays by the page! This concept will be reinforced in the exposition on the adage expounded in the next chapter, namely "It pays by the hour."

Of course, creating your own job is the ideal situation. Unfortunately, most of us do not have either the inclination or the skills to be entrepreneurs. Therefore we will always be tied to some job. While this book was written primarily for such people, namely the wage earners, it contains many helpful hints and ideas for entrepreneurs as well. It will also help the entrepreneurs understand the real world of corporations and business people whom they will have to deal with. I have found that successful entrepreneurs understand the real world quite well, and will continue to add to their knowledge of the real world. The unsuccessful ones do not.

Years ago when I graduated from college, in the early 60's which was back in the stone age of corporate practices, everyone wanted to be hired by a major corporation, such as IBM. In fact, IBM was often cited as the ideal corporation to be hired by, as it was believed that if one became an IBM employee, a good paying job for life with excellent benefits and retirement plan was assured. Further, IBM had a policy of quick and rapid promotions for those who were willing to become corporate persons. It was jokingly stated that IBM meant "I've Been Moved," but the belief that one became part of a caring and benevolent corporate family that would take care of one and one's family forever was certainly part of the corporate culture. The fact that one may have to put up with a few inconveniences, such as being moved frequently, was well worth the feeling of care and safety one received from the company. Further, being moved frequently was normally the result of promotions, and numerous perks to make the move palatable, indeed, profitable, for the employee, accompanied the moving process. These perks included such things as purchase of the employees house, generous moving expenses and allowances, aid with financing a new house, and purchase of automobiles if moving abroad, etc.

Many of my classmates did take jobs with corporations such as IBM, and a few still work for such corporations, but most do not. The reason most do not today is simple, THEY WERE LAID OFF in a corporate downsizing (sometimes mistakenly called reengineering). Corporate downsizing was a result of mergers, a result of business downturns, a result of the company's failure, a change in the corporation's business plan and markets, or for many other sound business reasons. These sound business reasons, of course, do not account for peoples feelings, hopes, and dreams, rather they are bottom line decisions based on the impersonal and unfeeling marketplace that the corporations operate in. For those who do still work for such corporations, the environment in these corporations is substantially different than it was when they were hired. The employees of these corporations are working under conditions of little or no job security, and are frequently working long hours to make up for the work done by the employee's who have been laid off. Further, in most cases, they have fewer benefits than they had when they were hired. In some cases they have been made contract employees with no benefits at all! Also, many have had to take de facto demotions due to the company downsizing, and a few have had to take salary cuts.

For those who were laid off, they usually found another job, but this job rarely had the job security or perks of the old job with the giant supposedly benevolent corporation. On the other hand, the giant supposedly benevolent corporation had to change itself to meet the demands of the "new" business environment and to survive as seen in the previous paragraph.

The bottom line is, the giant benevolent corporation is as dead as the dinosaurs, indeed, and no large corporation with competitors can afford to be a benevolent corporation. If it did, it would become non-competitive and would soon either go out of business or be adsorbed by some other corporation. If adsorbed, the absorbing corporation would soon change the employee policies to come into line with marketplace conditions.

Many of my classmates who went to work for corporations such as IBM found they had their dream job, for about ten to fifteen years, and then the marketplace and competition changed things. Thousands were laid off from

IBM in the 80's, and thousands more from major corporations such as Chrysler, Ford, General Motors, General Electric, Boeing, and the list goes on an on. In 1980 I went to work for a company that had been in business for over 50 years. This company claimed that they had never had a layoff. I thought that this sounded very good because I had been laid off twice before, and like most, I did not relish repeating the experience. Two years later, there was a significant downturn in that industry, and they had to lay off over 50% of their work force. There were people in that company who were in their 50's who had come to work for the company straight out of college. They had never worked for another company, and had never had to look for a job. They were recruited from college and expected a job for life. The emotional impact of being laid off in their 50's after working for the same company all their life was absolutely devastating for them. They did not know how to look for a job, had insufficient interviewing skills, and their own skills were suspect because they had worked for so long for one company. They were only a few years short of retirement age, and could not start retirement because they were not quite old enough. Most did not find a job, but were rehired later by the same company, either as a contract employee or at reduced salary.

> *So, after all, it really is true that "all jobs are temporary." Upon realizing the truth of this adage, how does one prepare oneself for the work force,*

and how does one ensure that there will always be a job out there to go to when one is laid off or the company has no more need of one's services for various reasons. Here are some suggestions:

- Find a niche to occupy
- Always keep your resume current
- Always keep abreast of developments in your line of work
- Observe the other rules of success.

<u>Find a Niche to Occupy</u>

Finding a niche to occupy is both easy and difficult. You want a niche that meets your skill capabilities, is not occupied by so many people that jobs are difficult to find, and is broad enough so jobs will always be available. As difficult as this may sound, most jobs meet this description, certainly all the better jobs do.

In general, finding a proper niche means that you need an education to gain entry into a niche that is not occupied by to many people. An example of a niche that is occupied by to many people is acting. I have a good friend who is an actor. He has two degrees in Drama and has attempted to break into the movie business several times. He has had bit parts in various productions, but has thus far been unable to generate sufficient money from acting to support himself. For this reason he teaches drama at a junior high school while trying to find parts in movies. Hopefully he will get the big break and be able to act in movies full time. In the meantime, he has had to develop a niche somewhat different than what he would like. Teaching is a niche for which there is a good demand for people. Even if he were to lose his job as a teacher, he would likely be able to find another.

In my own case my niche is environmental engineering. This business has also had its ups and downs, but there was always a job somewhere in this business. Because of the high educational requirements, there are a limited number of qualified people in the business. Because the business changes frequently and needs in this area change frequently, everyone in this business has had to move every now and then. I have worked for nine employers over a period of 34 years. I have been laid off twice, in both cases because of business downturns. In both cases I found a better job in a very short time. In both cases, I had to move from one city to another. I have actually worked in four different cities, and in all but one case the company paid for the move.

There is a niche for you too; you merely have to find it. Employment counselors and skill tests can be very helpful in this area.

Keep Your Resume Current

Always keep your resume current, and in most cases, it pays to have several resumes. Sometime during each job or project you are on, add that job or project to your resume.

In my business the company keeps a master resume for each employee from which a resume may be tailored to fit any job. The company does this because varying jobs have differing requirements. When preparing a proposal for a job, individuals being proposed to work on that job will have their résumé's tailored specifically for the position they are to occupy on that job. This is a common practice in industry.

Each time you find yourself looking for another job, you can tailor the resume sent with each job application specifically to that job. This means emphasizing the skills that you have that the company is looking for. Beware of over stating your skills. I have seen many resumes of persons who have done so, and we haven't hired a single one of them. Overstatement is readily apparent to the knowledgeable interviewer. Emphasizing your relevant skills though will greatly enhance your chances of obtaining an interview and later in obtaining a job offer. It will also usually generate a higher offer than a bad resume would.

Interviews are an all important part of the process. Behavior during an interview will determine whether you will be offered a job or not, and what the salary is likely to be. Read all you can on proper behavior at interviews, and be very careful about dress and personal hygiene. John Malloy of "Dress for Success" fame has some excellent suggestions in his books and newspaper columns.

Keep Abreast of Developments in Your Field

Most niches that pay well are highly specialized occupations. In this rapidly changing world it has been estimated by some pundits that a person has to learn as much every four or five years as they learned in college just to keep up. It has been estimated that knowledge doubles every ten years at this time in history. In my own business the technology, laws, rules, regulations, and other knowledge required probably double in less than that time, probably every seven years or so. The laws governing environmental matters undergo a major revolution about every ten years.

There is an old adage, "those that don't keep up will be left behind." There has probably never been a time in history when this hasn't been true, but it is more true today than ever before. Thankfully, there has also never been a time before now when information was more easily obtained and more cheaply obtained than it is now. I receive at least 15 technical magazines of which I pay for four; the others are free to the trade. The Internet has an astounding amount of information on it, most all of it free to users. Manufacturers of equipment readily give information on their equipment free, and will even send a salesman if it appears that an application is close.

One trade that has changed dramatically in the last few years is drafting. Draftspersons are no longer people that use boards, straight edges, triangles, and pencils; they are Computer Aided Drafting (CAD) operators. Drafting, like many other trades and professions, is now a totally computerized profession, and the pay and skill level required of draftspersons has dramatically increased. Further, the level of skill necessary to operate the specialized computers used in making drawings has increased exponentially, and is still increasing as more powerful and faster computers are being used and as software improves. Those who could not adjust to computers now have difficulty finding a job, while those who adjusted and developed computer skills are in great demand, and are earning very high incomes.

Again, the point is, keep up with developments, always know the latest buzzwords, and always watch for new ideas and technologies that can improve your position if you know them.

Observe the other Rules of Success

The rest of this book is about the other rules of success. One thought though involving pay. Generally your pay should increase on each subsequent job. While there are conditions that could cause you to have to take a job that would pay less than your previous job, always be cognizant of what you are worth going into any interview. You can find what you are worth through salary surveys and from other job offers from other interviews.

Chapter 2

It Pays By The Hour

If it doesn't, watch out!

This is a somewhat subtler adage than the first. The concept here is to obtain the maximum amount of money and benefits for your services. Since you have exactly as much time as everyone else, you will maximize your income by maximizing your hourly rate.

In the case of a salaried position, you have to take the salary and divide by the number of hours you are expected to work to obtain the actual hourly rate. Strange as it may seem, many a salaried person is actually earning less than the hourly employees they supervise (based on what they actually earn per hour of work) because the salaried person often works very long hours.

This concept has a direct impact on your decision as to which niche you decide to occupy. If you like to work long hours and make lots of money, then you should try for a job where this is possible. Generally, these are contract positions that pay by the hour and, in many cases, offer long hours. On the other hand, if you have lots of outside interests and like to spend time with your family, then you should try for a niche where you can work regular hours.

Generally, these are either salaried positions that do not expect a lot of (free) overtime, and these positions are becoming fewer and fewer, or they are time clock positions that truly pay by the hour based on a time clock. Most salaried positions expect substantial "free" overtime from their occupants. This is not necessarily bad as long as the salary is high enough to compensate for the "free" overtime. On the other hand, many hourly positions pay less than salaried positions, even when the "free" overtime of the salaried position is figured in.

There are notable exceptions to the generally accepted concept that salaried positions pay more. Some hourly positions that require extensive skills, such as aircraft mechanics and construction equipment operators for instance, earn high hourly rates and even higher rates for overtime. Many highly skilled construction workers earn more than doctors and lawyers and actually work fewer hours. Another example is CAD draftspersons that are hourly workers, but often earn as much an hour as their seniors in management, namely engineers. The engineers, however, are "exempt" and are essentially salaried workers with limited rights to overtime. CAD draftsmen are not "exempt" and are paid time and a half for over 8 hours a day and often work very long hours. Their paycheck is actually larger than the engineers who manage them. I actually knew one such person that worked 11 hours a day at his regular job where I worked, then picked up work from a job shop and took it home and worked until early the next morning. His hourly rate was nearly the same as mine, but he was paid time and a half overtime and had a second job as well. I was paid straight time for overtime and did not have a second job. No wonder he could afford a better car and house than I could!

Another alternative is working from your home. A few jobs and positions offer this possibility, and it is becoming more common as companies find that they can delete office space and expenses from their budgets by allowing people to work at home. While working at home appears attractive, particularly to those with small children to take care of, it carries some serious disadvantages. It does not allow personal interaction with one's coworkers. It does not give adequate access to office supplies or company records. It is harder to work at home than most people realize, given all the distractions there are in a home. A home worker will probably never receive the same confidence and trust that an office worker receives. This is because managers are inherently suspicious of workers, and will always suspect that the home worker is shirking.

Still another alternative is to own and operate a successful business. Successful small and medium sized businesses can earn their owners very substantial sums of money. However, with few exceptions, most successful businesspersons put in very long hours. I have a friend who successfully operated a landfill under contract for a major corporation. He owned and maintained the machinery necessary for the operation of the landfill and hired the operators and other help he needed to operate the landfill. At the end of five years he was a multimillionaire. He did however, work from 6 AM to about 8 or 9 PM seven days a week, and was on call 24 hours a day. Even so, his actual hourly rate amounted to the equivalent of over a hundred dollars an hour. Becoming a businessperson is a worthwhile alternative to consider if you are willing to put in the hours and have the ability and inclination to do it.

Every effort should be looked at from the standpoint of how much per hour does this job or opportunity really pay? Many doctors earn excellent salaries, but many work very long hours. This is true of many occupations. Be very aware of what you are getting into, and of what your needs and wants are concerning time. There are many jobs that pay well, but the demands on one's time are substantial in many of these jobs, and the actual hourly rate may not be very good.

The moral is to maximize your real hourly rate.

Chapter 3

Go for the money

They know what the job is worth!

Some years ago the company I was working for fell on hard times, and it became obvious that I would either have to leave or would eventually be laid off. I began a search for a better opportunity. At that time, I thought it would be good to get into business with someone else and build a consulting firm like the one I was working for. I in fact received such an offer from a man who had recently started a consulting firm and needed someone with my talents to handle the technical parts of the jobs he was able to sell. We signed an agreement which would have made me a partner in the firm after a year, and for the first time in my life I accepted a job that paid less than my previous job had paid, but had, I thought, better opportunities. I actually worked for this small five-person firm for about a year, but it became increasingly obvious that I would never become a partner. The founder simply was unable to psychologically accept anyone as a partner, and to this day the company operates as a small one owner-consulting firm. Although I was paid off in a sense, to vacate the contract, it was a mistake to have taken this job. I lost pay and gave up a year of advancement in another job that could have had at that time. I didn't "go for the money," and wound up regretting that I hadn't.

> *Given a choice of two jobs, all other things being equal, most people will choose the highest paying one. It is my thesis that the higher paying job is always the best choice. Unfortunately, all things are rarely equal. Most jobs offer various compromises between salary and other factors. A few of these factors are:*

- Working Hours
- Number of hours worked
- Overtime pay (or no overtime pay)
- Medical Benefits
- Child Care and other benefits.
- Opportunity for advancement
- Ownership opportunities
- Stock options
- Location
- Working conditions
- Expense policies
- Legal agreements
- Corporate culture
- Contract or regular employee
- Probation Period
- Retirement Plan

- Employee Policies

We have already covered working hours, overtime pay, and number of hours worked in previous chapters.

Medical benefits and a Retirement Plan are factors that must be considered and are part of one's pay. It is best to assign a real dollar value to these benefits and then add to the pay to determine what the job is really worth. Some firms offer childcare, and this is a very important consideration for some, particularly single parents. If one has a family or dependents and needs health insurance, or needs to plan for retirement, or needs childcare, benefits can be very important

Another option offered by many firms is the choice of being either a contract or a regular employee. Being a regular employee usually offers benefits and, in theory, greater longevity and stability, but as we have already seen, this is an illusion. A contract worker generally receives no benefits, but usually receives straight time and overtime pay at a higher rate. The benefits are worth a significant amount for most people, and in most cases, those who need the benefits are better off taking a job as a regular employee. On the other hand, I have known many persons who were quite happy as contract employees and would not take a regular employee job even if offered one. They prize their independence and ability to leave a job at will, and in most cases could get another job with no problem. They are often single and sometimes have difficulty getting along with bosses. Each individual has to decide for himself or herself, but for most the decision will be based on economics.

For many, opportunity for advancement, stock options, or ownership opportunities are extremely important. My sister is an IT professional and worked for a start up programming company for about a year. They worked extremely long hours and received part of their compensation in company stock. A few years later the company started trading their stock publically and my sisters stock was worth a very large amount of money, the company did quite well!

From my experience, ownership opportunities are rare, if you want to own a business, the best way is to start your own or inherit one.

How important is advancement to you? There was a major consulting firm years ago where it was joked that you advanced when the person on the drafting table in front of you dropped dead. You were then moved up to his or her table. Basically, advancement opportunities at this firm came through retirements and untimely deaths. That is, unfortunately, not uncommon. The opportunity for advancement is difficult to judge. In many firms, the position you are hired into is the position you will stay at the rest of your corporate life with that company. Advancement opportunities are a common promise by all personnel persons and by interviewers during most interviews. The reality is usually quite different. The best way to judge this is to ask other employees what the real situation is. Ask friends who know people who work for the company or find out where they hang out and go there. You will probably find out that the truth it is considerably different from what was presented at the interview. Many times, the only way to advance is to change jobs.

The location of the work can be important. In a large city, traveling from one side to another is stressful and time consuming, not to mention expensive. This must be considered in evaluating pay and benefits. Another variant of this is when one has to move to accept a new job, or when the company moves a person to a new location. Generally companies pay for such moves, but expenses that are allowed are sometimes meager, in part because of tax regulations, but some companies are very tight with moving expenses. The amount of moving expenses and the conditions of moving are considerations when determining overall compensation.

My father once owned a dry cleaning shop. Eventually he became allergic to the fumes in the shop and had to give it up. Working conditions are very important to many. Most jobs today are in offices where working conditions are basically the same, however, working conditions for many trades are very important. Is the work in an air-conditioned building or is one exposed to high heat or cold conditions? Is the plant dirty and filled with fumes? Working conditions can be a reason to not accept a job if the conditions will affect one's health.

Some jobs require a lot of traveling or other activities that generate reimbursable expenses. I knew a salesman one time that had to drive to appointments, some of which were a considerable distance from where he worked and lived. He received a mileage allowance for the use of his own car, but it was not enough to operate his car, essentially he was subsidizing the company and the excess car expenses were in reality a deduction from his salary. He tried many things to remedy this, including buying a used Volkswagen diesel car to reduce fuel expenses, but eventually he found another job. Expense accounts and expense account policy can be very important factor for some types of jobs.

Some jobs require employees to sign certain agreements for employment. A common such agreement is assignment of patent or copyright rights to the company. Thus if a person invents something the company gets the patent. This is normal in the engineering and scientific community because corporations are hiring such people to produce patentable and copyrightable products to sell. On the other hand, if you are inventing widgets in your garage and wish to preserve your rights you should look at these agreements carefully.

Corporate culture, which will be covered more thoroughly in another chapter, is an extremely important consideration in accepting a job. It is wise to observe this culture while interviewing, but it won't be completely apparent during an interview. It is OK in most cases to ask about corporate culture during an interview, and the answers may be quite illuminating. It is also prudent to ask others who work for the company off the record about the culture. Some companies have very strange corporate cultures; usually these companies are closely held family type firms. I have been interviewed several times by such firms, and was always rejected for the job. It was obvious to the interviewers that I would not "fit in" with the corporate culture. Had I been offered the job I would have rejected it because it became apparent to me, even during the interview that I would not "fit in." Even though all jobs are temporary, that was too temporary for me.

The moral of this chapter is to carefully evaluate all the benefits and liabilities of any job, and accept the best offer you can get. While all jobs are temporary, potential longevity is good if you can get it, there is no point in accepting a very short-term job unless it pays very well, or if you have no other choice, or you like or only need short-term jobs. If offered two jobs and one has higher total compensation than the other, then it is almost always preferable to take the higher compensating job. Employers know what the job is worth to them, so why take less than the best offer unless there is a strong overriding logical reason to do so?

Chapter 4

You never know who your next boss (or company) will be.

> *If you don't like your boss or company, wait a minute!*

> *I have worked for several companies that have merged with other companies, and, not infrequently, the merged company would merge with another company, and so on. The company I work for now has been merged several times, and recently merged with another company that I had previously worked for.*

It is a fairly common joke in corporate America that one needs to check the bulletin board when one comes to work to see what the name of the company is for that day. Mergers are almost that fast and frequent.

With all these mergers comes "restructuring," "reengineering," and the most dreaded word of all, "downsizing." As companies merge they find that they have two departments for almost all functions. There will undoubtedly be two legal departments, two personnel departments, two finance departments, etc. It is obvious that only one department is needed in each case, and only one set of supervisors for each department, so there is, as British say "redundancy." The extra people have to go, be transferred to other positions, or receive de facto demotions to lower positions. Other positions are scarce in a merged company, so that possibility is usually not available. Being demoted to a lower position means that a lower person must be laid off or be demoted, and somewhere along the job chain someone will loose his or her job. Further, the extra people will likely be culled in part on a salary basis so there are probably limited opportunities to be demoted. The reality is, if one is not going to be kept a layoff is inevitable. If one is going to be kept, the company may not do well in the future and those that are kept could face worse conditions. Indeed, both times I was laid off the company that laid me off fell on hard times and the kept employees faced lack of opportunities, reduced benefits, and no salary raises for a long time. On the other hand, I received a better job with greater opportunities. Being laid off is not necessarily a bad thing.

Regardless, whether kept or laid off, the worker could expect to have a new boss. And, given the pace of mergers and restructurings, the worker is likely to have a new boss fairly frequently. It is rare industry nowadays that does not turn over about every two years.

Now a few words about bosses. Bosses have a different agenda than their workers. It is supremely important for you to understand this. Indeed, a Boss has no other objective, but for he or she to appear to be a good company loyalist and for he or she to appear to be corporately politically correct to their boss, as well as fit in with the corporate culture. It is also important for the boss's department to appear corporately politically correct to the upper boss's. Note that the ultimate good of the company is not a concern of the boss. Regardless of where the company is going, good or bad, the boss will follow and enthusiastically support that path. A boss is not a whistle blower, and will suppress whistle blowers. More on bosses in the next chapter, where this subject will be covered in much more detail.

If you have a problem with your boss that can become, or is, an issue of company loyalty, corporate political correctness, or corporate culture, you have a much deeper problem that will probably not be solved by a change in bosses.

The same is true of the company. If you don't like your job or what you do then it is unlikely that a change in the company will improve your lot.

In both the above cases you should consider a change in occupation or other lifestyle change to achieve a higher level of job satisfaction and ultimate happiness. Only you know what makes you happy and gives you satisfaction with life. If you are not sure, there are many occupational counselors who can help and tests you can take to determine where you would fit best. There is no reason to go through life being unhappy about your job or your boss. The last chapter covers the issue of happiness more thoroughly.

The moral is, if you don't like your boss, or you don't like your company, but you like your job, wait a minute, or perhaps wait about two years at most, and they will probably change. Hopefully, you will like your new boss or company.

Chapter 5

Be willing to change anything.

Except maybe your sex!

Some years ago, in the heyday of equal opportunity, I worked for a consulting company that did primarily government work. It owned a subsidiary firm that did surveying work. A number of government surveying contracting jobs were offered that were subject to the equal opportunity laws. These laws gave preference to minorities and women in the award of government contracts. The subsidiary firm's president was a white male. It was jokingly said that he should get a sex change operation and take skin injections so we could get more work as a minority firm. While the equal opportunity laws were intended to provide opportunities for those who normally would not be given such opportunities, they also placed some stress on the firms that normally did the type or work that equal opportunity laws covered. A number of firms did, in fact, change their ownership so they could qualify for such work. The most common change was by small firms that were owned by a man. The man would give his wife 51% ownership in the firm then claim, quite legally, to be a minority owned firm. This gave the firm preference over non-minority owned firms for government contracts. This is one of the more obvious forms of change people are willing to do to succeed in business.

Another less obvious change is illustrated by the popular comic strip "Dilbert." Dilbert is always slyly out maneuvering his dumb pointy haired boss. The problem with this picture is Dilbert's boss has an entirely different agenda than Dilbert has, so the boss appears to be dumb, inconsiderate, and clueless to Dilbert. Be that as it may, Dilbert is not the boss, will probably never be the boss, and is frustrated by his boss's apparent stupidity. As noted in the previous chapter, bosses have a fixed and definite agenda, which they keep regardless of the situation or conditions. A boss is ambitious by nature, otherwise he or she would not be a boss, and is concerned only about how he or she appears to the upper bosses and about how his or her department appears to the upper bosses. Note that while a boss is a totally committed company loyalist, the good of the company is not a concern to the boss. A Boss will almost never be a whistle blower. The Boss's attitude is "My company, right or wrong." This is the attitude that made many companies great, but it is also the attitude the led to the downfall of several companies, among which were Enron and Arthur Anderson. Honesty and integrity are rarely an issue either with bosses; again the focus is on being loyal to the company and appearances. It was mid and upper level management fulfilling their role that brought Arthur Anderson and Enron down. Kenneth Lay, former president and CEO of Enron, claims to be a man of honesty and integrity, as will all boss's, but his actions, such as claiming Enron stock was a good buy and telling the employees to buy while he was selling, and other actions, show him to be a hypocrite of the first order. He was fulfilling his role as a boss, and he probably honestly believed what he himself was saying, but he and his company had departed from accepted business practices and were certainly a very long way from being honest and having integrity.

If you wish to be a boss and to achieve "success" in the corporate world, you must become like your boss, i. e. loyalty to the company becomes everything, and supersede all else. But be warned, in this day and age where the bottom line is everything and the pressure to increase shareholder value is immense, the probability that you will be required to compromise your morals and ethics assuming you have some, is very high. The compromising of your ethics and morals will not be a sudden "here it is" black or white decision, it will be a day to day wearing down of those ethics and morals as things get grayer and grayer. The fall of Enron started with one small act to correct a problem the bosses were unable to face, then another followed and another until the entire string collapsed. Arthur Anderson became intertwined with Enron in the name of making more money and expanding their operations. It appears no one in Arthur Anderson questioned if the companies growing conflicts of interest were a good thing for the company. Then the massive shredding of documents to cover up Enron's problems, which Arthur Anderson had failed to report, completed the fall of the company.

Some companies are much better at ethics than others. Companies that do not overly concern themselves with short term shareholder value, or more properly, are concerned about long term growth and want to be in business for a long time into the future are concerned about how they appear to the public in the long term. Such companies will emphasize a higher standard of ethics than quick growth companies. Such companies often have internal whistle blower procedures to detect unethical business practices. Some of these procedures are effective and some are not. Some are intended to ferret out disloyal employees. Generally speaking any company that has a system whereby an employee can contact the COE or President directly, either by E-mail or by letter, and can say anything short of a threat and not be fired, is an ethical company. This assumes, of course, that all letters or E-mails that concern ethics are investigated and properly dealt with.

As illustrated by the Enron and Arthur Anderson debacle, a renewed emphasis on ethics is the biggest change required today in corporate America.

Other changes to consider are elucidated in other chapters. A big change that could pay very big dividends is how you dress and how you look. Body language and mannerisms are all important in the business world.

Career path changes should also be considered. Often opportunities will arise in a slightly different occupation or job. While this may require a slightly different skill set than what you have, you can learn the needed skills.

Starting your own business should be considered. Most entrepreneurs are very adept at learning new skills and eventually develop a broad range of skills.

The moral of this chapter is that business presents a continually evolving landscape where change is the only constant. In order to succeed, you must be willing to change within the limits of your personal ethics and morals. Avoid situations where your ethics and morals could be compromised.

Chapter 6

Negotiate, negotiate, negotiate; everything is negotiable.

Well, almost everything.

Time after time in my life I have faced impossible situations where all seemed lost. Yet by negotiating and being willing to give on some small points I have saved the situation.

Some years ago I owned a house that was too small so we decided to have a house built, as it was cheaper to have one built than to buy a new one. We bought a lot and financed the purchase by getting what I thought was a swing loan from the bank. We put our house up for sale and some people contracted to buy it. The realtor did not understand the finer points of finance and set up the sale on a contract basis whereby they paid us rent to occupy the house and then had the right to apply the rent to purchase. Not realizing that this would be a problem we then contracted with a builder to build the new house. Late one Sunday night I received a call from a banker saying that they could not finance the new house until our house actually sold because we would be responsible for two house payments, which he could not allow. This put us into a bind because we were now faced with moving into an apartment for an extended time until the new occupants of our house decided to purchase it. Also the builder could not start on the new house until the old house was formally sold, delaying our move another six months or more.

I realized that something had to be done so I called the realtor and asked why these people simply did not buy the house straight away. He called them and found out that they had some CD's that did not expire for another six months so they could not buy the house until then. I knew that one could redeem CD's early but had to pay a penalty so I offered to lower the house price by the amount of the penalty, which was a few hundred dollars. They actually wanted to complete the deal as much as we did so agreed to that option. Thus with a phone call and a small concession I saved our new house.

We in fact had the builder start immediately and built the house under budget. I was moved four years later and we sold the house for 150% of what we had in it. Had I not done what I did the house would have cost a lot more, house prices were escalating rapidly, and we would have been stuck in a apartment for over a year.

Knowledge is essential in negotiating. You must know what the options are and what a fair price or position is. Time after time I have seen people take a hard stance and lose everything because they simply did not know what the situation was and what their options were. Just a slight amount of compromise would have gained them everything they wanted.

Another important point is professionals don't necessarily know what they are supposed to know. In this case the realtor should have known that the type of contract he advocated would mess up our house deal. He didn't, and his lack of knowledge cost me several hundred dollars on the deal. Anyone who has followed the advice of a stockbroker will soon find out that his or her advice is not necessarily good for the advisee. Stock brokers, like many others, make their money on sales and sometimes receive kickbacks in various forms from companies selling stock or funds. Several times I have bought funds on the advice of a stockbroker only to have the investment turn sour. I now do all investing myself with an online brokerage account that I control completely, and have done quite well. I won't mention insurance agents or lawyers, but you know the story, indeed, I have little doubt you have at least one or more stories to tell too.

A classic negotiating example everyone is aware of is negotiating to buy a car, one of the more traumatic experiences for many and one where the car dealer often makes much more than they should.

Many years ago I bought GM cars. I knew that the difference between the MSRP and sticker price and invoice price, the price dealers are supposedly charged, was 22%. This gave me great leverage, as I knew that I could negotiate the price to somewhere less than 22% off the

MSRP, usually I bought cars for about 20 to 21% off the MSRP. I no longer buy GM products, and haven't for many years for good reasons, but the situation has changed.

The difference between the MSRP and the invoice price now varies for different models even within a manufacturer's lineup. Fortunately, one can now find on the Internet all the information one needs to negotiate a good price on a car or truck. The Internet will give the MSRP, the invoice price, dealer incentives which are deductions from the invoice price for the dealer, and trade in value for your old car if you trade one in. Also, the internet will give the average selling price dealers get for whatever model you want.

Nowadays, I check the Internet then I walk into the dealer showroom and say, "I will buy a car for the internet price." Usually within minutes we have come to a negotiated price that is within dollars of the Internet price. Also, since I drive vehicles until the wheels fall off, so to speak, I do not trade in my old vehicle but rather either sell the old vehicle myself or let one of the "Sell it yourself" lots sell it. This eliminates the trade in value quotient to the negotiations, which is highly variable. However, if you are trading in a late model vehicle, then you usually save the difference in the sales tax, which can be a considerable amount. Thus with sufficient knowledge, you can negotiate a fair price for a vehicle with little effort.

Negotiating when accepting a job is sometimes necessary. Many things can be negotiated for certain positions, in fact for very high positions such as CFO or CEO, an employment contract is negotiated which spells out the terms of employment. But for more mundane positions there is limited to no room to negotiate. Nevertheless, if you have needs that need to be spelled out before you take a job you should negotiate to obtain these before you accept the job. Such needs could include leaving work early to pick up kids from childcare, days off for religious holydays, time off to take a sick parent or family member to the doctor, and so on.

It is best to negotiate such items with the firm AFTER you have been offered the job. Do not bring this up before you are offered the job as it could become a reason they might not offer you the job. After the firm has offered the job they have made a commitment and have said that they want you to fill the job. At that point they are most likely to negotiate and it is best to get the terms of work settled before you go to work. If you wait until you are on the job and, for instance, if the work hours are from 8 to 5, but you have to leave early to pick up kids or for some other reason, then you have started off on the wrong foot and have probably eliminated your chances for advancement and raises. If they know this in advance and have approved it, then there is no problem.

Most firms will allow a person to set their own work schedule, called flextime, within limits. Most companies will also allow employees with strong religious convictions to not work on their religious holydays, including the regular observance of a weekly holyday such as Saturday or Sunday. There are exceptions such as retail trades which depend on people working weekends and holidays, and certain types of work where a staff must be on duty 24 hours a day every day, or that depend on rotating shifts, etc. If you have strong beliefs that would prevent you from working under such conditions then you should seek employment in another area.

Another area that is negotiable, more often that not, is salary. Again, know what you are worth. The Internet is invaluable for information on what various occupations pay. Most large companies make a salary offer that is a take it or leave it type offer. However, many small firms try to control costs by paying staff as little as possible and will make a low offer initially. If they really want you it may be possible to counter offer a higher salary. You must know what you are worth in such situations so you can offer to work for a correct salary.

One of the annoying aspects of the negotiations between employer and prospective employee is "who goes first" when it comes to discussing salary. While many employers require the salary history of candidates, it's really the job seeker's business to know what they are worth. Conversely, though, a job seeker should be able to say what compensation he or she wants.

The next time you're asked to supply a salary history with your resume, it is recommended that you substitute a salary requirement instead. A statement such as, "I'm focusing on positions in the $90,000 to $100,000K range" is perfectly appropriate, and most companies won't toss your resume just because you say so. Most of them only want the numbers to make sure you're not too expensive for them, or too cheap [i.e., not qualified]. If your desired salary fits with what they're planning to pay a new hire, and your resume passes muster, you should be fine.

Many candidates hurt themselves by waiting until they have a sense of what the employer wants to pay before they speak up. They would rather let the hiring manager go first. That way, if the company is ready to pay $100,000, and they were only going to ask for $90,000, they haven't cost themselves money.

That seems reasonable, but you can waste a lot of time trying to get the company to make its move. More often, the recruiter or hiring manager will ask you [the job candidate] to go first -- for the same reason. If the expected salary range is in the 90s and a great-looking candidate says he's looking to make $85K, the hiring manager will be delighted.

What's the solution to this cat-and-mouse game? Ask the recruiter if there's a budgeted salary range for the job. If you can't get a number, share your salary expectation, while keeping in mind that if it's too aggressive, you may price yourself out of the running, and if it's too conservative, you may get an offer that's lower than you would have received otherwise.

Remember, as well, that your first offer isn't the end of the conversation. If you feel, later in the process, that you've underpriced your services, you can suggest a performance bonus on top of the base salary, or negotiate for other benefits, like tuition reimbursement, a car allowance, or more vacation.

You can't veer far off your original estimate; after all, if you've said "I'm focusing on positions paying in the 90s," it won't work too well to later say, "Now that I know you can pay $100,000, that's what I want." But you can negotiate for an earlier-than-usual performance and salary review. Or you can push for a sign-up bonus, a common way to raise a person's first-year earnings without disrupting the company's pay-grade system.

Suppose you get the offer but the money is disappointing. The thing to focus on is whether you really want the job; if you appreciate the challenge and the type of work. Assuming you do, your task is to negotiate a higher salary without being offensive. Here's what you say:

"Thank you so much for the offer. I'm really excited about the opportunity, particularly the chance to work with the great team you've assembled. We're a little way apart on pay. The offer is for $92,500, and I really need to be in the high 90s. Do you want to chat about that now, or share some ideas via e-mail or the phone?"

The key is that your goal is to negotiate. Don't sulk or get emotional about the offer; it isn't a personal insult. If you didn't share with the company what you wanted, that's your oversight. If you did offer a figure, or a range, and the offer missed it by more than a thousand or two, and that's a problem for you, you can legitimately ask: "Can you share with me your thoughts on the gap between the salary requirement I mentioned to you, the high 90s, and where you guys came in? Do you want to tie some of that to performance objectives?"

If a company misses the mark you set, the interviewer should explain why that happened. The person may mention established salary grades, or budget limits. In this situation, you have to become a salesperson, continuing to negotiate and overcoming objections. One way around a salary-grade problem may be a bonus instead of base pay to occur next year, if this year's budget has been exhausted. Once you know the problem, you can negotiate around it. Remember the key to successful negotiations is to determine the problem then come up with a satisfactory solution to both parties, or at lease a solution that both parties can agree to.

The worst way to respond to an unexciting salary offer is to say: "This offer is very low for my skill level" or otherwise turn the conversation into a shoving match. Your job was to sell the interviewer on your vast experience and skill, and if you didn't like the offer, you failed to do that!

If you like the offer apart from the compensation then it's worth your time to stick with the negotiating process and see whether you can turn it around. The right negotiation strategy can both get the starting salary where you want it to be, and establish you as a smooth negotiator a major asset for a newcomer on the team.

So here are five tips to get the money you want [or learn to live without it]:

- Focus on Solutions. Your message is, "I'm flexible." In lieu of the target starting salary, you can accept a sign-up bonus, an early review date, or a performance bonus at an agreed-upon time. Or maybe tuition reimbursement, a car allowance, additional vacation time, or any number of other incentives that would persuade you the job is worth taking.

- Listen Carefully. Pay attention to the company's explanation for the salary gap, and listen to the tone.

A hiring manager or HR person who says, "That's the best we could do," without further explanation, is really saying "Go take a flying leap." If they can't even talk about the constraints that are keeping them from making a better offer, it might not be a good place to work after all.

- Look at the Long Term. How long do you expect to work for this company, in this role, for this boss? If it's a place where you can make a difference, or is a great brand name for your resume, or if you would be working for a great leader, maybe a few thousand dollars won't be that big a deal. Your ego can quickly send you down unproductive paths when money is at issue, and that's a shame. Think about what two thousand dollars, once taxes are extracted, can buy you over the course of a year. If you cut down on the lattes, you could swing it. Further, it the company is that good and you are as good as you have sold yourself to be, you should move quickly up the ladder and will soon be making what you wanted in the first place plus possibly a lot more.

- Consider Trade-Offs. Think about "soft" elements you could trade against salary, if you need to. In a negotiation, if you give something up, you should get something. So the money isn't ideal -- can your title be improved? Can you get an account that you really wanted, or an international piece to the role? If you think about it, the money will come over time, or else you'll leave. What else about the job might be valuable or desirable?

- Turn the job down. If you feel that the gap is too great, walk away. The way to do that is not to show any ill will or resentment, just the opposite. Say to the recruiter or hiring manager [and then re-state, in the world's friendliest e-mail message to the highest-level person you met with], "I was delighted to meet you and the team. It seems like a wonderful opportunity, and I'm disappointed that we weren't able to make the dollars work, but I hope to stay in touch, and I wish you and the team all the best." Remember the adage that you never know who your next boss or company may be. They may reconsider and offer you what you wanted. It is also possible that the company you do go to work for will merge with this company and these people could wind up being either your bosses or subordinates? Don't make enemies; life is too short to worry about them.

Do this, of course, only if you can afford to walk away. But if you do, you may find that the company will reconsider and you get your offer, right away or in short order. All it takes is for an upper echelon manager to see your message and say to the hiring manager, "You let that clever Adrian Jones get away? What kind of delta are we talking about, five grand? That's ridiculous -- close the deal!"

In the worst case, which isn't a bad case at all, you'll part ways amicably, stay in touch, and circle back in the fullness of time to another opportunity in the same place. It happens every day.

As you think about your salary negotiation options, remember that the dollars are much more emotionally charged to you than they are to the employer. Don't take the negotiation too personally, or you'll put yourself at a disadvantage. Indeed one of the great mistakes made by negotiators is to get emotionally involved. It NEVER pays to get emotionally involved, always observe all things encountered in a negotiation in a totally logical emotionless way.

And, in the end, remember that what you get paid doesn't need to be part of what you share with the world, when you announce your new position at Gigantic Wonderful Company. That stays between you, your manager, and your checkbook. Indeed, there very few instances where it pays to let someone know what your salary is or what your financial state is. These few instances almost all involve banks and financial institutions.

Chapter 3 contains a list of considerations when evaluating a job opportunity. Many of these may be negotiable but others may not be. Companies usually have standardized health care plans, retirement plans, vacation, sick leave, holidays, etc. Negotiable items are usually limited to working hours, salary, sometimes raises, possibly advancement, possibly ownership opportunities, perhaps stock options, etc.. There is, of course, no point in attempting to negotiate any item that pertains to corporate culture or unwritten rules. These are cast in stone so to speak and you will be expected to comply with them regardless of your situation.

Chapter 7

Unwritten rules are more important than written rules.

> *Conformance with the corporate culture is everything. In fact, the written rules are frequently meaningless!*

If you want to see an example of how unwritten rules are more important than unwritten rules, simply go to any stoplight. When the green light changes to yellow, cars are supposed to begin stopping, only those cars that do not have room to stop are to go through the intersection. That is the written rule and is law in most parts of the world. What you will observe in most parts of the world, especially in the US, is that cars will continue to speed through the intersection, indeed, many will still be going through the intersection after the light turns red! Many cars will actually speed up when the light turns yellow in an attempt to get through the intersection as fast as possible to beat the red light. The unwritten rule is if you can get through the intersection before the light turns red, you are OK, indeed, since there is sometimes a delay where all lights are red, and it takes an instant for the drivers to react to a green light, you might even make it shortly after the light turns red. That is the unwritten rule that almost everyone follows. Here is an excellent example of how unwritten rules countermand and are more followed than the written rules. We have hundreds, perhaps thousands of examples we can observe every day.

In a corporation, there are many written rules, and the larger the corporation; the more written rules there are likely to be. One of the more common disconnect between written and unwritten rules are expense accounts. Written rules in most cases say a receipt is required for all purchases over $25, with some exceptions, and only certain types of purchases can be reimbursed on an expense account. These rules come primarily from the IRS although most companies have their own peculiarities. Nevertheless, one who obeys the rules to the letter, in most cases, will wind up paying substantially more out of their pocket than if they stayed home. For this reason there are various ways to add these expenses to expense accounts to keep even with the person's budget, and most who file expense accounts utilize these ways to do so. Indeed, most companies realize that this is happening, they would be a very poorly managed company if they did not, and tolerate it so that the employees will not feel they have been shortchanged. Most companies have a "yellow light" policy when it comes to written rules, and the higher up in management a person is, the more yellow the red light becomes.

Some years ago a lady who I knew from a previous company joined my company. She made the comment to me that she did not understand the corporate culture of this company, and indeed it did have a lot of unwritten rules. Further the management of the company had been very successful operating essentially using technical skills and common sense, some would say they managed by the eat of their pants, so to speak, and did not have a lot of written rules, relatively speaking. Thus the management had a lot of expectations that the workers would understand the unwritten rules and would abide by them, indeed the written rules in this case were largely ignored. This lady soon became discouraged and left the company. She was looking for a set of written rules she could follow.

Corporate culture is about unwritten rules and fitting in with the personalities that run the company. These two characteristics of companies go hand in hand, and one's success in a company depends largely on how well one understands and conforms to both.

In theory, anyone can follow written rules if they have sufficient incentive to do so. Those who dislike unwritten rules should go to work for a highly structured organization, such as the military or the government, although unwritten rules and especially personalities can play a big role on whether one succeeds in the military or government. Conformity is everything in such organizations. I have seen many a military person who has spent 20 or more years in the military have great difficulty adjusting to civilian life. Most go to work for the government to regain the structure and culture of obedience to written rules. On the other hand, some adjust quite well. Another place for such people is in utilities and service organizations such as UPS, FedEx, and other companies that are large service oriented companies. Service companies must have stringent written rules because the public sees their practices on an every day basis. If the FedEx or UPS person came by at any time of the day you might be concerned, but they try to be at a certain place at a certain time. If only the Postal Service worked as well! Unfortunately for those who are rule conscious, the path to advancement in such organizations depends on one understanding and conforming to unwritten rules, i. e., one who must have a written rule for everything, seriously limits their chances for advancement in virtually all organizations.

Conversely, those who understand and conform to corporate culture and unwritten rules will probably succeed admirably. Some examples of unwritten rules are:
- Loyalty to the company should be absolute.
- Loyalty to one's boss is absolutely necessary.
- Clients are the bosses too; nothing bad should ever be said about clients or their practices.
- Always appear to be following the written rules, even when you aren't.

- Adapt your personality to your bosses, and your boss's boss.
- Wear clothes like the others in your companies peer group, or slightly better clothes.
- Act like the others in your company peer group, only be slightly more enthusiastic about the company, your boss, and your clients.

And there are many more, they will vary with the company, and some companies have more than others.

Obedience to unwritten rules can be carried to extremes and can be unhealthy. Such was the case for Enron and Arthur Anderson. In those cases the corporate culture was so out of sync with normally accepted practice and what is considered ethical practices that it doomed two corporations. Personal ethics cause some people to become "whistle blowers." Becoming a whistle blower can carry with it a very high price. If wrong, or if others do not detect the practice being whistled at, the whistle blower is essentially blacklisted. Even if the whistle blower is vindicated, they will probably have difficulty finding another job because all prospective employers will be suspicious of them. A whistle blower gains a reputation of not being a team player.

Loyalty to one's company can never be in question if one is to be considered a team player. Most companies have mechanisms for people to disagree, but there are very sharp unwritten rules about how afar one can go with disagreement. Some companies have an "open door" policy where any employee can go to their boss's boss or to the company president and file a complaint. Some companies have E-Mail access to the president. As the joke goes, many former employees have written complaining E-mails or gone to see the boss's boss. Another joke says that the open door in the boss's office leads out into the street. One must have a reputation of being a team player and of disagreeing only within the limits of the unwritten rules. One must always enthusiastically support the company, even if one believes the company may be doing something one disagrees with. The same is true concerning one's boss and the company clients.

It is also important to give the appearance of obeying the written rules. It is an unwritten rule that you never say you has violated a written rule. Expense accounts are an example. You might quietly tell a fellow employee the correct method for filling out an expense account, but to proclaim to all that you put down $20 for a meal that you ate at McDonalds is not only bad form but can get you into trouble. The $20 might have covered not only the meal but also some other expenses you were not able to put on the account, which under the unwritten rules you can do. Of course, if the McDonalds is in Japan or some other high priced foreign countries, the $20 might be what you actually paid for the meal.

Every company has a generalized personality profile that most, indeed virtually all, in the company fit. Observe what this personality profile is and adapt to it. Your boss probably is the most successfully adapted person in your immediate circle, so adapting to his personality is essential. This is an unwritten rule that has disastrous consequences for anyone who does not obey it. Anyone who does not do this will find himself or herself very high on the layoff list, which, of course, does not exist, at least officially. If you believe that it does not exist I have a bridge to sell you. Another unwritten rule, to say the layoff list exists means one is disloyal to the company and is not a team player.

Clothes are all important. John Malloy in his book "Dress for Success" and in his newspaper columns continuously proves this with surveys and other data. In my company it is a written rule that all the salaried persons must wear a dress shirt, tie, and dress slacks, except on casual Friday's. The unwritten rule is that ties are optional, and most do not wear them. There is also an unwritten rule about casual dress. A nice sport shirt and Dockers or other designer casual clothes must be worn. To violate this rule by wearing lower class clothes, such as tee shirts and jeans, will move one up on the non-existent layoff list.

Conversely, those trying for a promotion should, as John Malloy recommends, wear slightly better clothes than their peers, i. e., in this case a tie, and perhaps, if one is really trying for a promotion, a sport coat or suit. This will also have the effect of moving one down slightly on the non existent layoff list. Of course overdressing can antagonize one's boss, so one must have a proper perspective on this matter.

Last but certainly not least, always be properly enthusiastic about the company, your boss, and the company clients. Those who are negative will definitely find themselves very high on the non-existent layoff list. Those who are over enthusiastic will come across as unbelievable and bosses will be suspicious. They will also find themselves on the wrong end of the list.

The moral is find out what the unwritten rules are and religiously obey them and fit in with the personality and culture of the company. If you have personal ethical problems with this you should either change your ethics or seek another company. If you observe things that are very wrong you may wish to become a whistle blower, but be aware that this action can carry a very high personal price tag.

Chapter 8

Get the big picture.

> *We live in an international corporate world, be international in outlook.*

We live in age where mergers and acquisitions have created or made almost all corporations international. International corporations and international business have and utilize different business practices and have a different culture from the old national companies. It is very important to understand this if you wish to succeed in the business world.

I work abroad frequently, have lived in three different countries, have visited nearly a hundred, and travel abroad frequently on business as well as for pleasure. I have friends and old high school classmates who have rarely or never ventured beyond the city limits or the county line I remember talking to one girl when I was in college from my hometown. I was thinking of asking her for a date. She then said she wanted to return to our hometown and live there the rest of her life. I decided immediately not to ask for the date.

There is certainly nothing wrong with my hometown, but it has very limited opportunities for success in my business, particularly in my line of work. I had no desire to return, I wanted to see the world and experience the things I had only read and dreamed about in college.

I work with many international oil and chemical companies, including Shell, Exxon-Mobil, Caltex, British Petroleum, Pertamina, etc. In these companies, multinational work forces work together to build plants, operate plants, make and transport oil, gas, chemicals, and a host of other petroleum based products. This international operating sphere is quite common nowadays. It is very important to learn to work with all nationalities. Indeed, perhaps the best hope for world peace is for all peoples to work together in international corporations.

I have worked in London with Brits, Nigerians, Lebanese, India Indians, Dutch, French, and Italians on a project being built in Nigeria by a consortium of companies with headquarters in the US, Britain, Holland, Nigeria, France, Italy, and Portugal. The project was to build a LNG Plant for a consortium of oil companies headed by Shell in Nigeria.

I later moved to Nigeria to help build this project and worked with Nigerians, Brits, French, Germans, Dutch, and Italians. The French were the Civil Engineers; the Italians managed the camp and provided environmental consulting services. The Brits were on our staff as the project was run out of our British office, the Dutch were managing the project for Shell, the Germans were the main Civil Contractor, and Nigerians worked for everyone.

On a project for Malaysia, I worked in Japan with Japanese, Dutch, Malaysians, Brits, and we even had one South African on the job. I, in fact, work frequently in Japan, and it is definitely one of the most interesting countries one can work in as far as culture is concerned.

I also worked in Cameroon with Cameroonians, Brits, and French. The Brits seem to be everywhere in the business world as are Americans. I have also worked in Australia with the Australians.

Americans are, unfortunately, woefully ignorant of foreign lands, peoples, and their outlook. Americans have a lot of misconceptions concerning foreigners, foreign lands, and foreign cultures. This is reflected in our politics and foreign policy and is why most foreigners like American culture, movies, and music, and usually love Americans on a personal level. However, they usually consider our politicians and statesmen to be a bunch of dangerous doddering dolts who couldn't find their hind end with both their hands. I read recently about a man that pedaled a bicycle through Syria, before the civil war, a country that in theory hates America and all Americans. He was greeted with great hospitality by the Arabs there and had a great time. He pedaled his bicycle from the Turkish border through Syria to Jordan.

Everywhere I have gone I have experienced the wonderful hospitality of foreigners. The more remote the area, the more hospitable people are. I remember a wonderful evening in a remote village in Cameroon with a French section manager of a French international construction company and his family. There was no hotel or other accommodation in this town so we had stayed in the Lutheran Mission. The evening was a wonderful break for us in an area with no TV and no other forms of entertainment.

The Japanese have made hospitality an art form. Once one understands the culture, evenings with Japanese businessmen are very illuminating and entertaining.

We had many wonderful project parties in Nigeria where one could talk to persons of almost any nationality. What tremendous learning opportunities these were!

In order to succeed in present international business climate you are going to have to:

1. Be tolerant of others
2. Be tolerant of yourself
3. Be tolerant of the culture and the country
4. Be tolerant of the company culture
5. Learn and respect other cultures
6. Learn the unwritten rules of the culture
7. In some cases try to learn other languages.

8. Learn the rules of travel.
9. Have a keen sense of awareness of where you are, who is around you, and who you are.
10. Understand where these people are coming from psychologically.

Be Tolerant of Others

This is the number one rule. In dealing with others, particularly foreigners, they are unknowingly going to offend you and your sensibilities. It is unavoidable. What is normal to them might be quite offensive to us, and vice versa. If you are very sensitive to others actions, you need to lose some of that sensitivity, as it will do you a disservice. The alternative is to stay in your hometown and never venture forth very far, not a very appetizing prospect to most of us. Further, you will have to do some things that might be offensive to you just to be sociable.

I do not like snails, crabs, shellfish, squid, octopus, and some other similar types of seafood, except fish, particularly when served raw. The Japanese love these. When in the company of the Japanese I try to eat everything they do and drink everything they do. One party served snails first. I managed to get the snail down as well as a lot of other things. Unfortunately, one of the courses was snail lips, or shavings from the edge of the snail shell. I have false teeth and simply could not chew these things. I apologized, explaining that my teeth would not let me eat these things, I did try, and they brought out some very nice raw salmon for me. I ate it with the proper expression of pleasure, I hope. Nevertheless, I thoroughly enjoyed the evening and learned a lot about Japanese cuisine.

The point is, be very, very, tolerant of others particularly those from a different culture than yours. Try to fit in and be sociable. As the saying goes, "When in Rome, Do as the Romans do." Probably no better advice has ever been given.

<u>Be tolerant of yourself</u>

Frequently, before leaving for a foreign assignment or before starting a multi-cultural project in the US Cultural Awareness sessions will be held. These sessions stress understanding and awareness of the differences in culture one is likely to encounter. In one such session the moderator explained that we would encounter "cultural bumps" as we interacted with the various persons on the task force. Understand that you ARE going to offend others sensibilities, probably many times as you interact. Learn to apologize when necessary, but then learn to forgive yourself for committing such a terrible blunder. Certainly you should learn from it and not do it again, but don't dwell on it to the point that you commit other blunders as well. Forgive yourself! Lose some of your self-consciousness!

Be tolerant of the Culture and the Country

When dealing with other cultures, whether it is in the US or abroad, it will help to understand that there will undoubtedly be some things or practices of that culture that are not acceptable in your culture. Be tolerant when this happens. In fact, Americans are far more likely to violate cultural rules than almost anyone else. That is because, relative to most cultures, we have very few hard and fast rules.

I have a friend who becomes quite upset when he is seated next to a smoker. Most countries do not have smoking and non-smoking sections in restaurants, hotels, etc. This same person will also almost always insist on having his food prepared in some special way, for instance he does not like Mayonnaise on his sandwich. Time after time in Japan he has instructed waitresses, who barely understand one or two words of English, to not put Mayonnaise on his sandwich. Every time the sandwich comes back with Mayonnaise. This is only one minor example of the "Ugly American." If he doesn't want Mayonnaise, he probably shouldn't be ordering sandwiches. I have seen Americans make terrible scenes in restaurants and stores because some little thing displeased them. I rarely, if ever, see other foreigners do that. Don't be the "Ugly American," if something displeases you and it is a minor thing, forget it and go on.

If my steak comes back rare because I cannot communicate with the waitress, I eat it rare.

There are many small things that can irritate foreigners, but they rarely make a scene when we violate their standards. We need to learn to be just as tolerant; indeed, we should be even more tolerant.

<u>Be tolerant of the Company Culture</u>

Be aware that in different countries conflicts and the decision-making processes are handled differently, and often in a much more formalized fashion than in the US. The Dutch and Brits, for instance, will have knock down drag out meetings to make decisions, often with table pounding and subtle name-calling. At the end of the day a decision is made and all go out for a beer at the local pub or alehouse.

The Japanese are quite different and very formalized. Only the boss makes decisions, but he will not make a decision until he has heard all sides. All will sit calmly around a table and give their opinion. The boss will then make the decision. If someone strongly disagrees they wait till the next team building social occasion, which will be in the evening and will involve moderate to heavy drinking. At that time anyone can approach the boss and tell him anything they want. The boss always has the right to change his mind and will frequently do so.

Another difference is in the US or Europe, it one needs information or needs to tell someone something, one goes directly to the person in charge of that function. The fact that this person may be several levels up or down on the organization chart makes little difference. In most cases, the others up and down the organization chart must be informed. Organization charts are mostly functioning guides.

In Japan, one must always go to the Manager of that section or group, then go down to the person, with the manager, who has the information or who can do what is needed. In Japan, the organization chart is inviolate; there is no movement outside of the chart. Everything goes all the way up the Manager, then to the next Manager, then down to the worker. The only time this is suspended is during the social team building night for that group. Since only the Managers group partakes of this social event, only those within the Managers group can utilize this route.

Learn the Unwritten Rules of the Culture

All cultures have unwritten rules. In Britain, for instance, it is a terrible breach of etiquette to not use the Queue or to get in line. In Japan, one is expected to take one's shoes off when entering a house and some restaurants and public places. Japanese prefer to use Kleenex tissues to blow their nose and consider handkerchiefs unsanitary.

Companies have even stranger unwritten rules sometimes. In Japan, most workers come into work between 9 and 10 AM; most are there about 9:30. They leave work mostly between 6 and 7 PM, most leaving about 6:30. Thus they work, for the most part, an 8-hour day with an hour off for lunch. There is no written rule that says that; it is the custom. Those who are ambitious will be there long after 7 PM, of course. I had a boss in Japan who seemed to always be in the office. I even went in one Sunday Morning to send a FAX and he was there! He was on the fast track up.

Try to learn the language

You will have an even more enjoyable time in a foreign country if you try to learn the language. Fortunately, English is the universal language of business, and most international companies use it as their official language. Recently a Swiss firm merged with a Swedish firm and decided to use English as the company language. That is how pervasive English is in the business world.

Nevertheless, learning the language will help to understand the culture and will give insight to the mindset of the country you are in. It will also make visits to local businesses and restaurants much more enjoyable.

Learn the rules of travel

Travel, like everything else, has written and unwritten rules. Experienced travelers know this and can navigate their way to almost anywhere using public transport systems. Fortunately, air and train travel has mostly written rules. You can carry so much on board a plane, check so many pounds of luggage, and you get on the plane in some sort of order established by the airline. Airline travel is fairly simple.

After airlines, things get complicated. There may be several ways from an airport to your destination. All these ways will take different times and cost different amounts of money.

For instance, one can go by train, bus, or cab from Tokyo to the airport, in this case let us use Narita as the airport. Tokyo is a substantial distance from Narita airport and a cab ride will likely cost in the neighborhood of $300 to $500. Buses cost $25 and will handle your luggage, a real asset if the bus leaves from your hotel, and many do, and take you to the airport. If traffic is bad though a bus can be late. Trains cost about $35, and require a $6 to $20 cab ride to the train station, will require you to carry your luggage some distance, which will include steps. Further, the trains have limited luggage carrying capacity and you must handle your own luggage. However, the trains will always be on time. If you are on a short business trip with little luggage, the train is the way to go. If not, then use the bus. Guidebooks usually will not tell you all that unfortunately.

Things are even stranger is some third world countries. Some airports have numerous checkpoints which require a fee (some call it a bribe) to pass. Thus the traveler can either pay the going rate for the bribes, or miss his or her plane. Becoming upset or showing anger could get the traveler detained by the police or worse yet, in a jail

Another hazard is cabs. In some countries cabs are not safe unless taken from a certain place. Taking a cab from somewhere else can get one robbed or worse.

It pays to obtain detailed information from someone who has been there, preferably several people who have been there to get the complete picture.

When traveling, get accurate information, never become angry, always smile, and be sociable.

Have a Keen Sense of Awareness

Understand who you are, where you are, and who is around you. You are first and foremost, an American, and you will be recognized as an American wherever you go. It is unavoidable; Americans are the most recognizable people on earth, even when they wear non-American clothes, if that is possible. Because you are an American people will expect you to behave in a certain way. These same people have observed both the "Ugly American" and the "Nice American." Be the "Nice American" and they will love you, trust me. Be the other and you could find yourself in jail.

Be aware of where you are. There are some places you don't want to be, and if you wander into such a place, get out ASAP. In third world countries it is often very dangerous to be out after dark, indeed it is quite dangerous to be out in the daytime in some areas of these countries. On the other hand, I have traveled through some very dangerous areas in Africa without incident. I have not taken any unnecessary chances; we knew what the danger was and how to avoid it. Also know what to do in an emergency.

In Africa, for instance, children and old people will often dart out onto the road. At night it is almost impossible to see them. We did not travel at night. During the day we kept the speed down so we could stop. If a person was hit the villagers would surround the vehicle and hack to death, with machetes, all of the occupants. The procedure if a person was hit was to speed to the nearest police station and hope they would protect you.

In another example, we sent a number of people to Vladivostok, Russia. Vladivostok has a reputation of being dangerous so it was decided that everyone should stay in the Hotel after dark. Two of the party, Japanese Gentlemen, were late from a restaurant and walked back to the Hotel in the dark. They had to walk through a pedestrian underpass under an intersection, and were met by some hooligans. They were beat up. They felt it was because they were Japanese, but our sources said the hooligans would have beat up anyone walking that way. The fact is, I would not go walking at night in downtown Houston, my hometown; it is not safe. It really isn't that safe even in the daylight in downtown Houston, but I walk there anyway.

The point is, Vladivostok may be considered dangerous, but it is probably no more dangerous than any downtown area in the USA. If you are aware of the danger and obey the "rules" you will probably not be harmed.

Understand where these people are coming from psychologically.

Last but not least, try to have an understanding of what the people from other cultures are thinking and how they think. A Japanese, for instance, is horrified if someone from a higher level comes to see him or her, without his or her boss.

In Nigeria, it is quite acceptable for a Nigerian to remove non-personal items from your desktop if they need it. Almost everything is shared in Nigeria among the tribal or family group. Their concept of private property is quite different from a European's concept.

At the other end of the scale, you could lose your wallet with a lot of money in it in Japan and probably get it back the next day, with all you money still in it. This, in fact, happened to a Canadian friend of my wife's. She left her backpack on a bus with her passport and about $500 worth of Japanese currency. She called her husband when she got home, she was married to a Japanese Gentleman, he called the bus company, and they had her backpack in lost and found. She went to reclaim it and everything was still in it, exactly as she had lost it, including the cash!

In the US, of course, if you lose your wallet the best you can usually hope for is to recover the wallet with the credit cards and other non-cash items still in it. The cash will disappear somehow. If you are not lucky, the credit cards and other identification will be used illegally.

While the above are extreme examples, they illustrate the fact that different cultures think differently about property, and many other things. When dealing with people from these other cultures, you must be as aware as you can be of how they think. Knowing that, you can effectively interface with them.

.

Chapter 9

Take all Difficult Assignments

It will look good on your resume even if success was not possible.

This may seem a strange bit of advice. Most difficult assignments fall into one of three categories. The first is an assignment that is so difficult that no one who takes the assignment is expected to succeed, except perhaps by dumb luck. The second is an assignment that is so difficult that only the best persons will be put on it. The third is an assignment so dangerous that it is difficult to find anyone to take it. Sometimes, indeed frequently, assignments fall into more than one category.

The true story is told of a man who managed a project for a large company. He lost $10 million on the project, a very large sum for the company. When he returned to the home office, he was called into his boss's office. When he got there he said, "I guess you are going to fire me?" His boss said, "Absolutely not, I just spent $10 million educating you." The man was very lucky he had such a wise boss. The boss knew that this man had learned some very valuable lessons. They were lessons, which should prevent a loss and should generate a profit on the next job. To fire the man and bring someone new in would probably result in another loss.

Another joke sums up this chapter. The story is told of the world's richest man who was being interviewed by several reporters. At the end of the interview he was asked what the secret of his success was. He said, "Good Judgment," then left the interview. A reporter was not satisfied with this answer and caught him on the way out. He asked, "How do you get Good Judgment?" The man said, "Experience." "But," asked the reporter, "How do you get experience?" The man answered, "Bad Judgment." The point is, all experience, even bad experience, is to be learned from, and the wise will learn from ALL experience. Indeed, one often learns more, frequently very much more, from bad experience than from good experience.

The first is the type of assignment that bosses like to put expendable people on. They figure the solution to the problem is let the person fail, blame failure on the person, and fire him or her. This way they get rid of someone they don't want and hopefully they will learn enough about the situation so the next person can succeed. If not, then the process is repeated until enough experience is gained to succeed, or the problem goes away.

The second type of assignment is the best type for the niche person. It is a difficult situation that falls into the person's niche and allows him or her to succeed using the unique skills. This assignment will make them seem even more valuable to the bosses and will enhance their position within the company. It will not necessarily lead to promotion however; indeed it probably won't result in promotion. It will likely lead to a raise in salary. The problem with specialized difficult situations is that they occur infrequently and present a very specialized skill set to the employer, which is more specialized than managerial skills.

The third type of assignment is so dangerous that no one will take it. Such an assignment could be, for instance, to a foreign location where there is danger from criminals or rebels, or from disease. A dangerous assignment should be very carefully looked at by the potential assignee. It would be good to interview people who have been there before to help you assess the risk. Proper assessment of the risk of such an assignment, then deciding how much risk you are willing to take is a difficult and involved decision. Years ago, I would take dangerous assignments, but there are certain types of assignments I will refuse now if there is real danger of certain types of disease or if there is real danger of being kidnapped, blown up, shot, or criminal activity is very high.

The first type of assignment is more interesting. A niche person should easily be able to handle the second type of difficult assignment. The third type of assignment is a function of how much risk you are willing to take.

The first type of assignment requires a skill set that no one in the organization has, and probably no one else in the world has. So why take such an assignment when it could result in dismissal. The reasons are not so obvious, but are very important.

A niche person who is able to think outside of the box has a much better chance to succeed in difficult assignments than a person who cannot think outside the box. Further, the niche person should have much more knowledge concerning the situation than his or her compatriots. In other words, the chance of success may be greater than perceived. But even if success is not achievable, the person who takes the assignment will gain knowledge at a rapid rate, and may be able to succeed the next time such an assignment becomes available. The interesting thing about resumes is, all experience is presented in a positive manner. Even if a person is perceived to have failed by his or her company, they have gained valuable experience that can be used on the next project or on the next job with another company. Further, the person may have actually succeeded on the assignment, but the success was not in terms that the company could quantify or measure. This is because the assignment was so unusual that the company managers did not have a method to quantify success, or were looking for one form of success where another actually occurred.

As an example of the first type of assignment, I took an unusual assignment on a foreign project. This assignment and job had never been done before by anyone. I succeeded in writing many plans and procedures for the job, most of which had never been written before. I succeeded in managing a lengthy and extensive environmental study involving 14 foreign scientists, five local scientists, and support staff. I obtained all the personnel and items they required, including a boat filled with very specialized scientific equipment, in a third world country where such items were thought to be unavailable. I also successfully obtained and organized the medical staff and set up the medical program for this project under very difficult conditions. However, after doing this a new manager came on site and removed me from my position because he thought my salary was too high. When I returned to the home office I was perceived a failure because I was sent back. In fact, the experience I gained on this job went on my resume and more jobs just like it opened up. Guess who was sent? I was, of course, because I was the only person in the company who had done that type of work, and was the only person who knew how to handle that type of job.

Dangerous assignments require very careful analysis and soul searching. I frequently accepted assignments to parts of the world where dangerous diseases lurked. I am very healthy and have a strong constitution. Nevertheless, some years ago I accepted an assignment to malaria stricken country. This was before some of the more effective malaria prophylactic drugs were developed. The malaria drugs given were Chloroquine and Paludrine, both of which had become ineffective against malaria. I did catch a low-grade form of malaria, and was unable to shake it until Larium came onto the market, a drug with significant side effects but at that time very effective against malaria.

About a year later I took an assignment to travel the length of another malaria-infested country and we were given Larium. This country also had bandits who commonly held up people on the roads, particularly in the northern part of the country. However, the company we were working for had quite good intelligence on the locations of these bandits. How they got this information I don't know but I suspect they had a number of well-paid informants. Nevertheless, one time we traveled all day on a back road, which was just a track through the jungle and bridges were two logs thrown across the streams. We did this to avoid a road that was known to be bandit infested. Most of the time we traveled by short take off and landing aircraft operating out of dirt strips cut out of the jungle, or by helicopter. These planes were refueled from 55-gallon drums, just like in the movies. The drivers of our vehicles would drive between bases and pick us up at the airfield.

Although Larium did cure my malaria, it had significant physiological and psychological side effects. I believe I have completely recovered from these side effects; however, there are some who claim that the side effects have lingered for them. Even though a drug may be available to cure or prevent the disease, it is advisable to check the side effects and see if it is acceptable for you to take. There are many diseases for which no known cure is available, so check to see if such diseases are endemic in the area of the assignment then assess the risk you are willing to take.

I managed an operation in Iraq for over a year from Houston, and was asked to go to Iraq on a long-term assignment several times. I had previously taken a vaccination shot for a disease for another assignment, and had a serious allergic reaction to the shot, so could not take the shots required for the assignment. I was not too enthused about the position in Iraq anyway and stayed in Houston to manage the project from that end. Later I did go to Iraq on a business trip, which did not require the shots. During the nearly two months I was there the camp I was in was mortared about every second or third night. Usually two or three rounds would hit the camp. There was no way to protect oneself at that time as they were in the process of building shelters, but since the attacks were random and at any time the shelters were pretty useless anyway. One could not live in the shelters. Later, things heated up even more and mortar attacks increased to every night and more rounds. Two weeks after I left the base three Pilipino workers were killed by a mortar round landing about 50 yards from where I was sleeping. My original assessments of the dangers of this assignment were correct.

The point is, difficult assignments are knowledge-building assignments; they expand one's skill set, and improve one's niche capabilities. Further, all such assignments, regardless of the outcome, can be made to look very good on a resume and enhance one's employability.

The moral of this chapter is; if the assignment is not too dangerous from a personal standpoint, it is probably a good idea to accept the assignment, regardless of the probability of success or failure. Like the joke says, sometimes you get good judgment from experience and bad judgment, but all can be made to look good on a resume because if the situation occurs again you now know what to do. Someone spent a lot of money training you.

Chapter 10

Always have a plan B, and a plan C, and a plan D, etc.!

Go on to bigger and better things, or, if at first you do not succeed, try, try, again (usually somewhere else).

It is important to have a plan for your life. It is said that if you don't know where you are going, any road will get your there. Unfortunately, "there" may not be a place you will like. The plan should include a plan to make you happy and to generate the income you think you will need for that happiness. Unfortunately, those who have little money are more likely to be unhappy than those who have a good income, although there is not a direct link between income and happiness. As the saying goes, "Money can add to happiness that is already there, it cannot buy happiness."

I have always had a plan for my life. This plan of necessity changes when major life events dictate.

When I was a boy, my Boy Scout Troop collected old newspapers and magazines to finance Troop activities. We collected papers from door to door, and usually collected in the better parts of town, as they had the most paper. The people in these parts of town had very nice houses and nice cars, and obviously were making very good salaries or incomes. I wanted to live like them and have what they had when I became an adult. I noted that almost all had college educations so I decided I wanted to go to college.

I had a talent for math and science so I decided to be an Engineer. I decided I would like to be a Mechanical Engineer. Unfortunately, I could not get a scholarship for Mechanical Engineering, but I could get a scholarship to become a Civil Engineer. Plan A, Mechanical Engineering, did not work so Plan B, Civil Engineering, became the plan. The overall plan was to obtain a college degree in engineering, so a slight deviation was OK.

If I had not received a scholarship I still planned to go to college somehow, and I had saved enough money by working part time after school to pay for slightly more than a year of college without the scholarship.

Have a plan, but let it be a plan that is broad enough so minor deviations won't hurt. Later on, when I was in my senior year, I received an opportunity to go to graduate school, paid for by the U. S. Government. The government needed Environmental Engineers, so a program was instituted to train such engineers. It looked good to me so I deviated a little again and became an Environmental Engineer.

I enjoy my job immensely, I am past normal retirement age, I still work, and I do not want to retire. My job is a very rewarding job from a personal standpoint and is more than sufficiently rewarding from a financial standpoint. I am not, however, a company president. I rose to the position of Manager of Health, Safety, and Environmental Affairs for large, greater than $1 billion, projects for a major engineering and construction company. I controlled the expenditure of $5 to $6 million dollars a month on some projects.

I have written several published books, including one on Industrial Wastewater, that is accepted as a standard in the business and was, financially, very profitable. I have also written 20 published papers and consider myself a success. I am what I wanted to be. I practiced what I am preaching. It does work.

You can be what you want to be to, but you will never make it if you don't have a plan.

In formulating your plan please be realistic. You have talents and abilities. However, if you do not have a talent for math and science, for instance, there is no point in trying to become an Engineer or Scientist. There are, however, many other things you can be, such as a Lawyer, businessperson, etc. Also please recognize that certain occupations, such as rock star, motion picture star, etc, are very difficult, but not impossible, to achieve. I have a friend, who is an actor, and he is a good actor, but he has never been able to become a star. He teaches, does bit parts, and hopes. Hopefully his break will come some day, but he is now in his 40's. He does like his life though and is quite pleased with what he has been able to do.

The point is, some occupations are going to be difficult to enter no matter how hard you try. Pick something you will be happy with. Life is too short to be unhappy.

Another caveat, picking a narrow field for your vocation may or may not be a good idea. The world is changing so fast that new vocations appear almost daily, and many old vocations become obsolete almost daily. Actually, most vocations soldier on as niches. For instance, a little over 100 years ago horseshoeing was a viable occupation that many engaged in. Nowadays, there is still a demand for a few horseshoeers, but not anywhere near the number that used to ply the trade. Radio and TV repairmen are still around, but the days when there was a repair shop on almost every corner are gone. People throw away old radios and TV's. The technology changes so rapidly that it is not worth keeping an old Radio or TV set.

Some years ago I wrote a book titled "Biblical Living." This was more a labor of love intending to elucidate some of what I had learned about the Bible rather than an attempt to write a best seller. This was fortunate because the book did not sell well. Nevertheless, I included in this book the results of years of study and collecting information on how people live long and happy lives. There are certain characteristics that identify those who are likely to live longer and be happier than others. You can acquire most of these characteristics yourself and achieve what these long-lived and happy people have done.

Studies have shown that life and quality of life can be extended if you do the following, which are in an approximate order of importance:

- Socialize; this is the number one factor in quality of life and health. Even people in poor health will live longer and better if they socialize with others. Socializing reduces stress as well. Church is primarily a social group, so it is no wonder that people who regularly attend church or synagogue have been shown to live longer. Paul's admonition to "forsake not the assembling or yourselves together" has health implications. Of course, socializing with a fraternal or other social group will achieve the same results.
- Control fats in your diet and maintain your correct weight. Overweight persons shorten their lives significantly, further they are generally in poorer heath. A study of centenarians showed that not one had ever been overweight. Unfortunately, there are some people who have a genetic predisposition to being overweight, and unfortunately, my family falls into that group. The good news is that there is good (HDL) and

bad (LDL) cholesterol, and my family also has a genetic predisposition to have the good cholesterol. People with this genetic predisposition for HDL live significantly longer than those without. Of course, if we can control our weight, we will live even longer and better.

- Drink the equivalent of 4 to 6 oz. of wine or equivalent a day. Seventy-two scientific studies have shown that this will not only lengthen your life but will significantly reduce the probability of disease and will make you feel better. This is one drink or 2 beers a day. Another study showed that drinking only one glass of red wine a week would significantly reduce your chances of contracting cancer. In general, red wine is the healthiest alcoholic drink as shown by several studies. Of course, drinking too much has significant negative health effects, and those prone to alcoholism should abstain. All the nations except 2 above the US and under Japan on the longevity lists are European. The other two are Israel (23) and Australia (2). France is number 3 on the list. The French live 3.1 years longer and Italians (6) live 2.7 years longer than US people do primarily because of wine drinking. Australians, number 2 right behind Japan, who are very fond of beer and drinking in general, live 3.2 years longer than US people. Moderate drinking reduces cholesterol, improves circulation, reduces aches and pains, and improves health and attitude in general. My doctor recommends it.

- Exercise, my doctor says walk 3 miles a day, and my friend Toru-sans doctor says 10,000 steps a day. Actually, I bought a pedometer and I usually do make a total of about 9600 steps a day when I get my walk in. That's about 6 miles. I recommend that you buy a pedometer to see how much exercise you really get. They are cheap and the new electronic ones are very good.
- Take an aspirin a day, this improves circulation and helps the heart. It has also been shown to lower the bad cholesterol. My doctor recommends it but check with your doctor before doing this.
- Have a "spirit of adventure." Psychologists who have studied people who have lived a long time have found this to be THE common denominator. This means being open minded and always learn about anything you have the opportunity to learn about. Learn from others, especially those of other races, lifestyles, and religions. Be open to new ideas. Nowadays, you can sit in a chair and surf the Internet and learn. You can broaden your social contacts. You don't have to travel or have a lot of money. Be inquisitive about everything. Negative (closed minded) people live significantly shorter, unhappier, and less healthy lives, a proven statistical fact.
- Avoid stress, and good luck on that one. Perhaps how you handle stress is more important, since stress is unavoidable. Here is where "true religion" which brings "enlightenment" can help. A lot of things are

not quite so important when you understand the universe and how you fit into it. In general, moderately religious people handle stress better than non-religious people, although those who are very deeply (immoderately) religious can lead very stressful lives as well. A Christian sage, namely Paul, plainly advocated "moderation in all things."

- Take vitamins with nutrient supplements. My doctor recommends it. One a day Wal-Mart or K-Mart brand vitamins do just fine. I think I bought 300 tablets for $5.98 last time.
- Don't smoke. Smoking significantly reduces life span and health, and pack a day smokers live an average of 7 years less than non-smokers. Smokers have significantly more health problems than non-smokers. Studies have shown that smokers are at less risk for Parkinson's disease, but at higher risk for the other diseases. My first wife's mother smoked one cigarette a day. She lived longer than most of her brothers and sisters. I attempted to find statistics on very moderate smoking and was able to find only two studies of significance. Most studies used statistics extrapolated from heavy (pack a day) smoking statistics, which would be the same thing as taking statistics for heavy drinkers and extending to light drinkers. I. E. if a person who drinks a quart of booze a day has a 100% chance of getting Cirrhosis of the Liver, then one who drinks a 3.65 quarts a year has a 1% chance. It just isn't so, in fact the person who drinks a drink a day has

virtually no chance of contracting Cirrhosis of the Liver and will be healthier and will live longer than one who doesn't drink at all. Fortunately, we have statistics for all kinds of drinking habits separately. I find it somewhat odd that neither the cigarette companies nor the government have done any research on this, however, in a sense, it would be negative research from their standpoint. There have been only limited studies on second-hand smoke, but these, believe it or not, have been mostly inconclusive. I looked at the actual data and it cannot be concluded that second-hand smoke does or does not cause negative health effects on non-smokers around smokers. One European study showed no effect of second hand smoke on children where one parent smoked, and only a slight increase in risk for the non-smoking parent. More studies are needed. A Japanese study showed that non-smokers can be affected temporarily by second hand smoke, but did not explore long term effects. I believe that there may be two sides to this issue, as Native Americans used tobacco as a healing herb.

The End

Epilogue

Murphy's Laws

Murphy is a mythical Irishman who formulated a series of pessimistic and sometimes sarcastic laws or rules. Perhaps unfortunately, these rules have a ring of truth to them. The basic rule is:

Whatever can go wrong, will go wrong.

Other laws are as follows:

- Anything good in life is either immoral, illegal, or fattening.
- It is morally wrong to allow suckers to keep their money.
- The light at the end of the tunnel is the headlamp of an oncoming train.
- Celibacy is not hereditary.
- Never sleep with anyone crazier than yourself.
- Beauty is only skin deep but ugly goes to the bone.
- Never play leapfrog with a Unicorn.
- A Smith and Wessen beats four aces.
- If everything seems to be going well, you obviously don't know what the hell is going on.

- Never argue with a fool, people might not know the difference.
- A short cut is the longest distance between two points.
- Friends come and go but enemies accumulate.
- Everyone has a scheme for getting rich that will not work.
- The other line always moves faster.
- Murphy's Golden Rule: Whoever has the gold makes the rules.
- The race is not always to the swift nor the battle to strong, but that's the way to bet.
- Anything you try to fix will take longer and cost more than you thought.
- The repairman will never have seen a model quite like yours before.
- In order to get a loan, you must first prove you don't need it.
- No matter how long or hard you shop for an item, after you've bought it, it will be on sale somewhere cheaper.
- The chance of a piece of bread falling with the buttered side down is directly proportional to the cost of the carpet.

Murphy was an Optimist

Authors Information

Ralph L. Stephenson, BS, MS, PE, is a professional environmentalist who retired from his position as the Environmental Manager of a multi-billion dollar engineering and construction company with worldwide operations and projects. He has traveled extensively and managed environmental issues for projects in dozens of countries. He is an internationally recognized expert in environmental science and technology, and is presently writing science fiction novels with the theme of climate change. These visionary novels give scientifically based projections of the effects of climate change and the configuration of the coming post-climate change world.

He has written ten non-fiction works. Two are graduate level engineering textbooks, several self-help books and two books about the Bible, one covering money and economics, and one an exegesis. All books are available on Amazon.com, Kindle.com, Createspace.com, and from the author. The five science fiction novels currently available are:

1. The Confederation Galactica
2. Toy Boy and the Astrologer
3. The Second Expedition

4. The Tentacles of Time
5. Nothing is What it Seems
6. The Lion of Lade, a historical novel about Vikings
7. A Matter of Survival, coming in 2018

Non-Fiction works of general interest currently available are:

1. My Family – Plunkett, Clore, Steele, and Stephenson. A history of my family, homesteading, and Kansas.
2. Publish Free!!!. How to publish your work on Amazon's Createspace and Kindle for free.
3. Biblical Living. A book about what the Bible says about how to live our lives.
4. Home Bartending Made Simple. How to stock a home bar and make mixed drinks.
5. Common Sense Gun Control. The middle ground for gun control with common sense proposals to keep guns out of the hands of those who misuse them.
6. Common Sense Doomsday Prepping. How to prepare for the Apocalypse.
7. Sell it on the Internet. Turn trash to cash by selling on the Internet.

8. Memoirs of the Second Gulf War, or How the plan to reelect a President destabilized the Middle East

9. The Seven Religions of the Bible, An Exegesis of the seven religions of the Bible.

10. Ralph's Rough Rules for Success.